THE WATERS OF BIRMINGHAM

Brian Lewis

PONTEFRACT PRESS
September 1997

Published by:	Pontefract Press
	17 Linden Terrace
	Pontefract, WF8 4AE
	tel. 01977 793121
	fax 01977-690916
	e-mail: brian@pontefractpress.demon.co.uk
© Text:	Brian Lewis
© Cover Image:	Richard Battye
Cover Design:	Ann Battye
Page Design:	Reini Schühle
Printing:	FM Repro, Roberttown, Liversedge
ISBN:	1 900325 08 X
Classification:	Poetry

For Ernest Hall of Dean Clough
who bought a derelict carpet mill and
turned it into a practical Utopia

and

John Baskerville of Birmingham
who, having made money japanning,
made costly experiments in letter
founding and produced type faces which
have scarcely been excelled.

CANTO ONE - RAIN

In which Jude arrives at New Street Station and goes up New Street, through Chamberlain Square and to the Central Library. There she studies the statues of the Floosie In The Jacuzzi, the Sphinx, Queen Victoria, Thomas Attwood and the Iron Man; though not in that order. That done, she swallows hard and counts to ten before setting out on a journey to find a lost river.

Brummagem rain will seep down to the bone
and dampen all you've got from Loveday Street
to Deritend. Life's drizzle-wrapped down here. You stand alone
in Colmore Row to wait a late night bus and then retreat
through rain.
                    Yet it is rarely puddle spiked or gusts
into your face like hail. Slow, persuasive, it is there
because it is; the rotting Midlands rain that rusts
the breast of each Iron Man who sides Victoria Square.

Jude has arrived in rain. Her collar's held pinned
close beneath her chin. She ventures forth, goes round about,
wandering through Birmingham. Siberian wind
would take her breath away, this drizzle won't. Doubt
penetrates, doubt like constant rain. So much she knows,
she travels northwards with one change of clothes.

If you've a proper job and rise at half past seven,
take Sainsbury's muesli and the slimmer's toast
at eight, go workwards, have a desk, then at eleven
take cappuccino from a red sachet, you are the ghost
that haunts a girl like Jude. She wants to saunter from a city shop
swinging a light bag, *Rackhams* emblemed on
- gold leaf and black in classy lettering - to stop
at chic Viyella, to have a man who's put upon.

She wants a Barratt house, or maybe two,
in far Kingstanding, a laser printer, a telly
with a dish, utility room, also a downstairs loo,
for rainy days a vestibule for her welly-
bobs - another for the garden hose - a granny flat;
a widening world with *welcome* on its mat.

Journey out to any big estate, the Newtown one
will do. Look to the bedroom window, then ask why
the curtains at high noon are closed; why, all alone,
a woman on a bed continually switches channels. The Sky
's her limit and the sun dazzles her screen, her dreams
reflect back to the bed she calls her pit. There's little rhyme
or reason in what that woman's at. She has no schemes
to wake her, gets up at cool eleven; if she has the time.
Look at the bricks that lie about with mattresses and glass
upon the green. No painted Maypole here, a wedge
of sanitowels perhaps. No one walks this grass
though there are acres, unless it is to scuff the edge,
to tread in hardy annuals close on the tarmacked path.
This is a council joke so give a civic laugh.

Charity does not begin at home but in a charity shop,
remember that, oh Hospice shoppers. On Harborne High each
empty shop has rags-once-riches clothes, that cheapo stop-
me-and-buy gear purchased for pence. All in easy reach
when stylists' labels have been scissored out
so you cannot return. Look if you are in doubt.
Places have labels too; Digbeth-Deritend is Inner
City Brum, so is Ladywood and Hockley Brook;
Edgbaston's sort of, though with trees and dinner
time placings in silver service. Somewhere to look
upon, see how the other half lives.
                                            Greenery breaks
through into the City's labels: Selly 'Oak',
Small 'Heath', Acocks 'Green'. Each name awakes
a meadow. So much has gone.
                                  I'm sorry that I spoke

but can't you see what we are doing? Today there is a chance
to change the world around, go tipsy-turvy - left hand down,
gears into reverse - and learn to park anew. The song and dance
of progress brings memories on.
          'I shop around and go up Town
most days, Hardly anything's the same one day to the next.
New Street changes daily. The Theatre Royal
has gone and where did Hudsons stand? The sub-text
is the sight line, that doesn't change.'
            Brummies loyal
to earlier traditions are left to wonder where the
buses went and how they turned up Corporation
Street and came to rest by Lewis's.
           'In forty-eight me
and me mom would shop at Grey's, buy a creation
in Christian Dior's New Look, for on the whole
we thought *Bon Mode*.'
         'Baby, you saw the good times roll.'

Jude's coat lacks any label, so who is this
girl? What does she seek, why does she wander? A clue
please, just one titchy clue.
                        No mother now will kiss
her pain away.
                An orphan then?
                                You
might say that, although a stalwart mother lives
way in the North, for choice she don't go back
and see her all that often.
                        An alienette who gives
and takes?
                Yes, that's her style. She cannot probe and hack
her way to friendship, autistic almost. Come what might
she first will introspect and, after counting ten, will analyse.
Not showy but unsure, has laddered tights.
                                        A lady of the night?
No, though she stands and thinks on the kerb side.
                                        It can't be wise
at her age to Lil Marlene that way?
                        No definitely, it is not.

You've talked of Jude but have you learned a lot?

She's travelled serious distances?
                              Up to a moon
of Saturn looking for a wedding ring?
                              Not quite that far.
To Smethwick, then via Dudley Road? She could soon
be there upon the eighty-two. The Seventh Star
which ends the heavenly Plough is clearly seen
when resting on Cape Hill.
                     She needs a break. Too care-
worn for her years, if you ask me. I have been
watching her. I want to know what makes her
tick and all I see is youthful weariness. Just look
at her jacket, stitching won't save nine. It's only fluke
her raylon belt is any use, for see the buckle's broke.

If you ask me, this Judy simply needs a bloke.

'Not so,' thinks Jude - this Jude can read our thought -
'A cod fish needs a Raleigh bike before I reach my
marriage time. Oh Fiddle-de-dee.'
                                      Her mother taught
her several golden rules: 'Wedding is a bring-and-buy
time for a girl but pick-and-mix for men,
so best avoid,' a cynic mother she. 'That butterfly wings
which flutter in Peru bring rainbows to our shores, then
we experience chaos.' There's two.
                                    Most things
she taught, Jude did not rate. She thought a famous four
the font of wisdom, that *All you need is love*,
that peace deserves a second chance and at the core
of most things there is kindness.
                                  'Heavens above,
think that and you'll think owt. I really pity
her naivety.'
                Like most, Mom sought a fabled City.

Is great Brum fabulous?
            I'll say it is, for there are
squares with clear fountains and a rare gardener's Babylon
hangs from the Central Library front - mind, it's tiny. Care
is taken to balance stark modernity with horticulture. 'One
you cannot have without the other,' or so the old song says.
That song Jude hums as on her mindful pilgrimage
she makes her way up paved New Street. Eight ways
lead to the central square which is the focus of a Golden Age.
Let us name some.
                    Edmund and steep Pinfold Street,
the streets of Paradise and Waterloo. The square
with the crystal fountain built to honour Chamberlain, neat
as his monocle but very Gothick. That one's a snare
for tired shoppers who seek the sun and quiet water.
That fountain is the spindle of the cultural quarter.

The road name where she stands is iron cast.
New Street it says in black on grubby white.
A dependable sign if ever Jude saw one. It will last
this century out and one more too. It is just right
for where it stands. Look at the road sign.
Think of the name, think Brummagem. Brum, say it twice.
Brum-brum, Brum-brum. Can you hear the engine
turn? Listen: 'Brum-brum.' Brum has no asking price.
Observe her closely. Jude is no rustic down to see the lights
but a modern miss wanting to find change. She won't stand still
for long. She walks to the Town Hall, sets her sights
and then looks back to High Street. Once a green hill,
high above a sandstone church, it now is locked in space
by concrete roadways.
                         A bull ring was the market place.

Jude pauses, has a vision. A bull is standing by
a river chomping grass. Taurus is her star sign,
perhaps this is her beast, her strength, the reason why
she's stopped and left the homeward train. Divine
visions are Jude's stock in trade. This cosmic bull
has milk-white flanks as wide as Africa, and in between
its horns a disc of soft Welsh gold, sad eyes, a full
forehead, he is no numb skull but a wonder. She's seen
nothing more clear than this Bull in all her dreaming.

Back to Victoria Square. Here one style blends
with that next to it with unassuming grace. Clever scheming
planners have made this place from scrag ends
that were passed down from an earlier civic age
of Municipal pride, an age of certainty and robust courage,

then added some.

                     Inherited is a Jubilee Queen,
who never was a mite amused. They've let James Watt
and Priestley stand as courtiers. Wee Jimmy has been
plastered startling white, and Oxygen Joe's got
done up smart in burnished bronze. Tom Attwood
sits upon the steps - he's bronze as well - seeming to make
a meaningful point to couples who ignore him. Blood
flows around their veins, not his. This Thursday, their take
and give of love is very mortal. He is not. Their food
 - finger to finger, tongue to tongue - cannot sustain
his argument. The square's a pivot for the Good
and Powerful - great themes refreshed by rain.
'Gracious me, confronted with such monuments retain
some street cred. Without it,' thinks Jude, 'I strive in vain.'

The season has just started. Brum City's midweek match
kicks off this very afternoon. Stolid men with shaven heads
and royal blue scarves trog the streets in droves. 'Watch
it,' thinks Jude, 'following groups of silent souls leads
nowhere unless you have a point of view; a motley crowd
is not a personality on the move. You could easily be caught
out if you jumped to that conclusion. Walk tall, be proud,
don't be a daft happeth or a saft supporter.'

               Jude had been taught
to trust herself and not to trust in much, support no one, least
ways not a team who rarely win away.

                  She's not a lot to say
on modern things.

       Conventional?

            No, pinned on her breast
there is a scarlet ribbon. There'll be the devil's own to play
if Mom found what that favour meant. Mom's ignorance pained
her. Right uptight was Mom.

          And still the City rained.

She watches silent walking men, thinks, 'Drove
suits this lot. Effers and blinders, yet only a tenth has wit
enough to drive for profit.' They are supporters who for love
of Birmingham mouth home and away, sit
in cold stands on Easter morn, shout: 'Shoot the Ref!'
'Off-side!' and 'Bugger me!' Each one a slave
to his own goal. She listens to the counterpoint: 'Eff
this, eff that.'
              'They are four lines short of a stave,'
she thinks. 'Their dominant melody is crass, pretty
naff really. They're Chorus when all's said and done,
armorial bearers, simpletons, supporters of the City.

And close-by is the Town Hall where Mendelssohn
conducted *Elijah* and Handel was performed in a blaze
of gaslight. *Here sheep will safely graze.*'

If the Queen read Jude's thoughts and laughed
that would be a comic how-do-you-do for sure.
Victoria won't do that. She's serious. Real hard graft
built the robust square, that's why her outlook's dour.
She disapproves of floosies and of modern choice,
bits-and-bobs newly imported. Also the core
funding, for it's European. See her point. It's not nice
to have a nubile goddess in a stone jacuzzi at your
feet if you are Empress of India and confidently expect
to rule the world some day. When Gormley's Man
invades your space as iron knight you naturally detect
a slight. There's no obvious decorum. There is a plan
of sorts, there always is, but where's it to be found?

Think what you will, it's Jude who stands on solid ground.

Jude looks about her. Likes Hansom's brave Town Hall,
Palladian style. The Council House is different; overwrought
with more detail than is needed. 'I'll pay that place a call
some day,' she thinks. 'I bet the inside's brill.'

                                                            She's taught
herself a menu of smart things. Architecture's one of many
she has studied; but then British libraries are free
so you can wander in, key computers, read most any
book. Astrology interests her, so does the statuary you see
in public places. Birmingham excites her, for it is grandiose
and public to the point where outrage merges with serene
sophistication. Designed so that not even a patriotic religiose
with a shoulder chip could be offended: a much respected Queen,
a sphinx with ears and one without, steps, cascades of water
a couple in a fountain; a son kneeling facing a daughter.

Although in many ways a loser with no label in her coat
Jude had retained from Sec Mod school a thing or two
which she holds to as sacred; eh gee: 'Don't gloat
when other folks are down, your time will come.' - 'Do
unto others as you'd fancy for yourself.'
                                                     There also was
a model she was taught about in Human Geography
called 'How A Pigeon Sees A City'. She liked it because
it hinted order and belonged, a straight apostrophe.

The model was a nest of circles centred on an eyeball point
called Central Business District. Around this focus went
a splattered hoop of factories and sheds, a clip joint
or two, a natty nightlife club, sidings, an area sent
to try us if we planned ahead.
                                    Come, when all was done
even with statuary, cities are chaos, they never are a bowl of fun.

A man with folded raincoat neat upon his arm
approaches her as she stands wondering. 'How do,'
he says. His voice is flat as Colmore Row. 'Did I alarm?'
He clearly didn't. This was just his way to show
he'd welcome speech with this young lady. She
smiles. That is enough. He has an opening. 'Precisely
what are you looking at?' He smiles, all teeth. 'Round here we
say *How do*.'
                              'Thanks.' She also smiles, 'Just nicely.'

Jude listens to his speech, its timbre's all its own.
Nasal, flat, but with a small curve on every edge, and a
crisp cackle for a laugh; droll almost, a monotone
which holds you. She thinks, 'Brummies can say
anything as long as they don't laugh. They're sharpened on the knife
used to stir Macheath's concoctions. What a zest for life.'

Jude liked the phrase, 'How do.' - 'How do you
do,' perhaps? A truncation of a greeting made
shorter to accommodate the space you speak in, two
words instead of three. In working towns, words get splayed
about in space and bitten into; thus used, they don't convey
the best of sense there is. In Yorkshire it's 'Now, then,'
which greets a labouring man.

                        'It is' is now just 'It's.' - 'Okay'
becomes OK *vowel and consonant in Caps*. When
precision goes for a Burton - Brum, Brum, Brum - we swop
and change at will yet keep the little courtesies intact.
Castrate those and the vocal pitch begins to rise an octave. A lop
job if ever there was one, but sometimes recommended. In fact
this is the reason why the ancient man prefers Ern to Ernest,
Bri to Brian, Trace to Tracy. The full name is for Sunday Best.

Our words are playful joys, are Lego bricks which move
and grow to glowing Hyatt Towers of new expression
above a desert made of grunt and groan. Jude is in love
with words. They're totally fascinating, so no concession
gets given. As grammarian Jude is merciless, so will bend
vocabularies until they fit, thinks, 'The ancient Brummy gent
uses all his words sparingly but the younger end
spice their speech and forge words which get bent
to chance's horseshoes. Language is additive. A Bengal
spice or a tuberous vegetable from Trinidad/Tobago
have entered. A Brummy vindaloo's on call
and can be served. Never apologise, for the vocabularies on show
speak of a revolution.'
        Yet the older end grow bitter,
ask, 'Who speaks the Glorious Qur'an and the Bhagavad Gita?'

The square's a dictionary of stylistic odds and sods.
Its modern navel is Great Floosie, belly of Europe, eyes
of Astrakhan. The Iron Man is Tuxco, the gods
who shaped him stalked the Andes. Close by, a wise
sphinx guarding steps. She might be from anywhere. It could be
the citizens of lost Atlantis that first saw those thighs.
Having watched the Kraken wake and seen the Three
Horsemen of the Apocalypse ride the sun set, sighs
within the sand stone moved her and, as ash fell,
she gave up dreaming. This sphinx has learnt to swim
through stark necessity. From there she's been to hell
and back and knows how far it was. Her mate - she met him
as the earth moved - has settled here with her, a staid
couple who don't go anywhere, just watch folk promenade.

'Do you like our Floosie?' said the man whose name
was Ern. 'She's Birmingham's spirit of abundance.
This big factory tart's fecundity is symbolic and her fame
parades the wonders of the city. It's not by chance
that she is naked and inviting. A true daughter
of this city. What's on show is less than what's for
sale. But then you probably know that.
                                        Clear water
brims and flows over her open hand, for at the core
of any mystery there is always generosity. Some think
that Brummagem has lost its way, its enterprise
lost in squandered opportunities. Not every link
has to be forged here. There is vigour and surprise
which comes in from elsewhere. Do we need parades
and promises? This is the fabled City of a Thousand Trades.'

With that he went.
                        Jude must appease her gods
with regular gifts. Most things you need are in your pocket.
Jude searches hers for small change. She is at odds
with life so finds there crumbs of crisps.
                                      The locket
round her neck's a special talisman. She takes it off
and as she lays it on the ground upon the roadway
thinks, 'I know my place. I must not cough
or smirk, for this is not the back of nowhere, decay
does not limp in this great square.'
                                      There's scarce a breath
of wind, yet as each crumbling falls it finds its place
within a perfect circle.
                        'A river flows beneath
these city streets through dark brick culverts. That space
holds mystery for a girl, therefore I'm bound to trek
along on pilgrimage, explore and chance my neck.'

The talisman's spot centre. Around it lie the crumbs
of comfort. Close to it stands a Northern girl who has
arrived yet has not found her dwelling place. Thumbs
down has been her destiny up to this hour. What was
it Mother said? 'Don't go too far,' and now she's done
just that. She's reached a city that she does not know
and made a target from the bits she has. Standing alone
outside the circle she wonders really what she's at. Till now
she's followed where the crowd led; followed folk down dale,
up hill. Always seen the urban life as simple calculation
on acting after a short pause.
         'All other rules pale
into insignificance compared with the ten seconds rule. My station
in life is determined by decorum and precise measurement.
It is a golden rule worked through by me yet heaven-sent.'

Jude pours a viscous brown libation from a cola can
and makes her vow. The Town Hall's classical so she'll use
the words that Roman Matrons used; the vow a woman
made who travelled long upon straight roads. (Choose
as she must, she can't run out on history.)
                                                    'I praise
the genius of this place and ask for help both
from the nymphs and lesser city gods. To them I raise
this modest loving cup and offer with my oath
a maiden's greeting. Give me Joy this day and keep
me safe and fit for work as I this journey take.'

That done, she swallows hard and counts to ten. Steep
steps lead down from Central Library.
                                        'To make
it this far when you're cautious is enough.
I'm moving Forward.'
                        She gives a nervous cough.

CANTO TWO - THE BIG ISSUE

In which Jude wonders about the Big Issue. In Paradise Forum she confronts Poverty and sees for the first time the Hyatt Tower. Books are above her when she thinks about technology, radicalism, the Lunar Society and why Birmingham was once the City of a Thousand Trades.

Beside a door that opens on command a black man stands;
a solitaire, he sings, 'Show me the love I have
been waiting for.' Passers-by ignore him.
                                            The bands
he once admired left charts long since and now he'll only shave
upon Sundays when God sleeps in.

                                        Jude nods as she goes
to the door into the Paradise Shopping Mall
but he sings on: 'Show me that love' - most days he'll choose
the same lament - 'I have been waiting for.'

                                              'Thou shall
not covet this man's theme,' thinks Jude. 'It's all
he has, a phrase born out of just a hint of hope.
Assertiveness, pride, injunctions to walk tall
have all but passed him by; that's why he sings. You cope
if you've a solitary line of song. And this one
does, he's strong.'
                              Jude knows his type. He is a man alone.

'*Big Issue*' shouts a girl who stands beside the man. A ragkin
she, one who holds her dog in check by showering it
with guilt. She's clearly unemployed; long legged, thin
as bulimia, awkward as spite, (also as innocence,) she's wit
enough to stand, and sense enough to move
along if asked. Is active in her search for work; but still
can't find it anywhere.
                          And her possessions?
                                          The treasure trove
she has is in a box in Selly Oak. (More of that box anon.) Will
she triumph; hear Brum-brum inside herself?
                                                Her back
is to the Mall so she can't see the flimsies in the Knickerbox
or panty hose which hangs in flash Sock Shop. The rack
on which she lies is Benefit. She does not have the pox,
yet as she looks at you, you can detect her growing fear.

She hums the *Issue Song*.
                            We do not choose to hear.

She sings the *Issue Song* yet who can really know
just what the issues are, when week by steady week
they all converge? What was the sacred cow
of yesterday is now on hold. Jowl by pitted cheek;
Employment and Housing. Which issue must
government take to the top? What social song sets
people free? All are real questions.
                                        'Trust
in yourself,' thinks Jude, 'rain comes as frets.'

Big Brum bells on the hour and starlings fly away
in droves, shitting as they go, to sit upon a ledge
hard by a bank which at a year-end promises to pay
a regular dividend of eight percent. That pledge
is made as cumulus clouds form the horsemen War
Disease and Hunger.
                    Our Jude stands, face towards the door.

'Open Sesame,' she commands.
On this, the sliding door
of Paradise glides on its guiding rail but when she's entered
it closes to entrap her. 'I get caught in words, for
wallowing in my ignorance my world is 'I'; I'm centred
on myself. My hand is to the plough, I break new ground, import
into my scheme of things ideas, when ideas suit my moods.
That's how I know Big Mac's a star sign, a sort
of double portal to the nether world of processed foods.'

'Why do we categorise?' thinks Jude. 'And why do doors
slide on a running rail to burn up energy when triggered
by a beam? They seem small miracles but aren't.'
Eight floors
above lies 'Precious Books'. Jude counted them, figured
out their place within the scheme of things.
Jude: 'Thus far
so good. Seven plus one. The Plough points to the Northern Star.'

Paradise Forum is the mall Jude looks upon and trogs
into. First thing she finds are tourist stands with folding
A4 sheets.
                These list events: show-trials for docile dogs,
a Mahler Symphony or two, the Exhibition Centre. Holding
in her hand the centre fold and looking down Jude sees
that all are *Joys Of Man's Desiring*.
                                    'This is a pleasure
dome,' she thinks, 'a place where people choose to please
themselves, have fun. A market place to take at leisure.

Here we emerge as fripperies and in that re-creation
slough off old skin and learn there isn't very much
between the lower and the middle class. If wise beyond your station
you will learn to upwardly aspire until you easily touch
the upper crust. Accent and taste are the costume jewellery
of style, diamanté brooches worn as fashion's foolery.'

That said, it is the time to enter in and walk the Mall,
taste of the food and drink that is on offer, sup Diet
Coke or a Tango from designer cans. *Thou Shall*
and *Thou Shalt Not* has no place here.

                                          Folk in the Hyatt
do not eat of this vacuous food but eat far better fare.
Food's offered on a gilded platter inside that mirrored tower.
There are mints set beside the till, receptionists seem to care.
(Mind, waiters bow you in and set you up, then on the hour.
declare you a midnight Cinders from Perrault's *Land of Fable*.)

Look at the contrast. A hotel faced with glass
where you can see yourself reflected in the table
or else a plastic shopping mall; little between. (Class
distinction gets sanctioned as we shop.) Here
and there hints of what we'll see when the skies grow clear.

'Books are high above me, they are above us all if you
think through, yet here they soar above the Mall.
Like stacking trays the floors reach up. What's true
is at the top, while down below there's novels and tall
tales of derring-do, and in between a fabulous display
of written erudition. Each book's a crusted jewel.
The Seventh Star held fast inside the Milky Way
I hold in trust if I read on. That's why I play it cool.
Each time I take a text and snuggle up I feel the virtuosity
of myself enter to another's brain and import in the signs
of my own longings. I have Enlightened curiosity.
My search for Truth goes well beyond the ley lines
and Tarot cards into infinities of Precious Books.
There Truth resides for girls, it's never in their looks.'

Above the Mall stand plaster saints, sods and odds
who each day recognise indulgences the Tarot Popes
gave freely. No Bull Ring this. The trash of nature, pea pods
and cabbage stalks, have no place here. Various dopes
get dealt by junkies on the exit brig but inside
dealers have a Camelot pavilion, a kiosk painted white
and day-glo red. Here from a stool a wide-eyed
virgin acolyte sells scripts to wistful travellers. Here tight-
budget single mothers even have a chance to win. (Of course
if an odd Faraday came your way then you would
have the right to have a flutter too).
         Even the Bourse
cannot create the tension of the six ball game. What could
compete with this chance in a million?
           The floor
is litter free, the purchasers are for the most part very poor.

The flutter of a butterfly in far Peru breeds hurricanes,
remember that and count your every cost. Before you buy
a script and mark six of the forty-nine, weigh up the gains.
Search through the wherefores, for the primal Why
of simply being you. Each of us marks cards. Chance
is the water where existence floats, it is not in the pain
of struggling to achieve but in curiosity that you glance
the reason why we're here when walking through the rain.

She wonders, should she take a Livery Street long-shot
chance and buy? When travelling to the end
all odds get very long. Think deep on chance then slot
into your scheme a set of tragedies. Ask, 'Why spend
good money?' Simply buy a pair of shoes.

That's logical.
                      Face it, we have the right to lose.

That is because we have the right to take a chance,
have a free will.
                     'Beware,' thinks Jude, 'although I have
some choice which route I take, it's next to none. The Dance
of Death is marked upon my card. Quite soon I'll leave
the Palais, yet when my number's up the show goes on.
I know my heart beat is a simple clock set to alarm,
which signals both my end of time, also the con
that's always took me in. Being mortal I can come to harm
if I play fast and loose with Karma, with my fate. All
is ordained, each minute, every second, has been planned
long, long ago. As one who's heard the siren call
of ova beckoning solitary sperm I understand
the grandeur of small matter, and comprehend creation.'

As she thinks this her brows knit into concentration.

A stable girl like her needs a recurring dream that she
can latch onto. Jude's dream concerns a river
but whether that river is inside her, is the key
to clearer understanding, she's not made out. *Giver
Receiver, Returner* is its litany, a constant lap
of water on a muddied strand. That is what she hears;
a steady lap, lap, lap.
                         The water from the tap
is not the water that she's dreamt about the years,
on from her infancy to now. That's water at command.
The water that she dreams of is another sort. Water
of our African origins, the Serengeti rivers that fanned
the High Veldt, that tide: daughter, mother, daughter;
the tidal rhythms, the broken waters of the first birth.
Water that falls as rain to slake the thirst of Mother Earth.

The Mall sells tack and coloured ties, sells painted boxes
and the oriental silken shoes; kitsch in infinite variety.

This five foot up from where Enlightened doxies
in crinolined folderols waited for the Lunar Society
to emerge and walk their Paradise Row.
                                            'Where lads who own
flash bovver boots now stand, their vacant brains
as empty as their open mouths - 'Tom's up in town' -
a flash of wonder once lit a Midland sky.'
                                          Jude entertains
that thought, for Science quite excites her. No empty scratch cat
she. She knows the Apple Mac, Pee See and what
a Corel Draw can do. She wanders on the Web and at
the most appropriate place logs on. She sees that
Science rested here awhile in 1774. She's come to know
the Lunarists sat here.
                              For this was Paradise Row.

She knows she stands on hallowed ground. A revolution
started here two centuries since. Upon the night
of the full moon wise men came seeking the solution
to practical questions. Answers were argued round a table right
here on this very spot. Lunatics of logic here found threads
to lead them to tomorrow's market place. This was some array!
Atheists, Friends, Utilitarians; men without established creeds.

Jude names them: Josiah Wedgwood, Baskerville (a
special favourite he). Boulton, Murdoch. She knows that
on this very spot Science entered an engineering shop
and went Brum-brum. She thinks upon James Watt,
Boulton's partner at Soho. He was a Scot, a top
instrument maker, a Glasgow engineer
who aped cosmology with his *Sun and Planet Gear*.

What remains of their discoveries?
                                      Easy that, this Brave New
World.
          Nothing was the same again. Since Science is the light
that searches gold in increments new capital can accrue
and bring the logic forth to build Jerusalem. These took delight
in knowing what the offers were, then mixed and picked.
Who ever can say exactly just what each one came to know?
Knowledge has cogs and moving parts. Yet here ideas clicked
as revolutionary Europe stirred: Rousseau, Voltaire, Diderot.

Jack Baskerville was buried in his own back yard
- here's few know that - standing bolt upright,
a candle to the Great Enlightenment. It's hard
to think of greater heroes than John Baskerville. Quite
the philosopher that one, but also chemist, poetaster
print designer, historian, and in his day, a writing master.

Joe Priestley was a friend. A Royalist mob burnt down
the Priestley home. They smashed retorts and the blown jar
he used to distil elements. They placed a paper crown
upon a bust of Thomas Paine and called him 'shithead'. With 'Ah
yo watch this our kid,' they threw into the flame
The Rights Of Man while in his private library above
a woman pissed upon a book. They thought that learning was a game.

Then there was the Doctor, Erasmus Darwin. He wrote *The Love
Of Plants*, echoing Linneus in erotic verse, botanic poetry;
chuckling as stamen and pistil came together, reproducing
in coded couplets sexual jokes, ordering all into a symmetry
of natural selection. A lively book. Excellent for seducing
Art through Science. In his blood stream hints of evolution.

Birmingham's was a Reasoned Revolution.

A real Big Issue, our *Sun and Planet Gear* is Ignorance.
We don't see how the words, once honed, are in decay.
Our lack of curiosity's another. Because of that trance-
like state our mind instructs us to retract the delay
mechanism of our brains. The caution which made us
search the perfect word, hold off, then find
it still within the breath of time, the fuss,
the wish to know, that now has almost gone. We lag behind.

We hear 'Big Issue' when walking New Street but never analyse
beyond the poverty trap. We think the late night
bus from Colmore Row has left us standing and in surprise
stare after it. We've lost resilience, can't tell what's right
from all that's wrong. Standing in rain we fail to suss
the ignorance which has become a part of us.